Stories from Many Lands

Collected By
Judith Pasamanick

Illustrated by
Carol Hudson

Modern Curriculum Press

ACKNOWLEDGMENTS

WHAT KIND OF BIRD IS THAT? by Mirra Ginsburg. Copyright © 1973 by Mirra Ginsburg. Reprinted by permission of the author's estate.

"The Knee-High Man" from THE KNEE-HIGH MAN AND OTHER TALES, by Julius Lester. Text copyright © 1972 by Julius Lester. Reprinted by permission of the publisher, Dial Books for Young Readers.

"The Chinese Red Riding Hoods" from CHINESE FAIRY TALES by Isabelle Chang. Copyright © 1965 by Barre Publishers. Reprinted by permission of Crown Publishers, Inc.

"A Wolf and Little Daughter" from THE PEOPLE COULD FLY: American Black Folktales by Virginia Hamilton. Text copyright © 1985 by Virginia Hamilton. Reprinted by permission of Alfred A. Knopf, Inc.

"How Spider Got a Thin Waist" from THE ADVENTURES OF SPIDER: West African Folk Tales by Joyce Cooper Arkhurst. Copyright © 1964 by Joyce Cooper Arkhurst. Reprinted by permission of Little, Brown Inc.

"The Three Petitions" from THE TIGER AND THE RABBIT AND OTHER TALES, by Pura Belpre. Copyright © 1965 by Pura Belpre. Reprinted by permission of the author's estate.

"The Noise in the Woods" from THE TALES OF UNCLE REMUS: The Adventures of Brer Rabbit by Julius Lester. Text copyright © 1987 by Julius Lester. Reprinted by permission of the publisher, Dial Books for Young Readers.

"Mockingbird Gives Out the Calls" from PEOPLE OF THE SHORT BLUE CORN by Harold Courlander. Copyright © 1970 by Harold Courlander. Reprinted by permission of Harcourt Brace Jovanovich, Inc.

"Miss Mouse Finds a Bridegroom" from BURMESE AND THAI FAIRY TALES by Eleanor Brockett. Copyright © 1965 by Eleanor Brockett. Reprinted by permission of the author's estate.

"The Bed" from THE TIGER AND THE RABBIT AND OTHER TALES, by Pura Belpre. Copyright © 1965 by Pura Belpre. Reprinted by permission of the author's estate.

Every reasonable effort has been made to locate the ownership of copyrighted materials and to make due acknowledgment. Any errors or omissions will gladly be rectified in future editions.

Design: Ade Skunta and Company
Project Editor: Marty Geyen
Associate Editor: Mary Ann Porrata

The folk tales in this book come from many people, from many parts of the world. Some of the stories were told in other languages before they were written in the English version. Some of these tales will make you laugh. Others will make you wonder what will happen. All of them will make you think!

So after you have read the stories, think about this question. How can it be that people from different parts of the world can be so very much alike?

Table of Contents

This first story is an old Russian folk tale about a very unusual goose. It's a good story to read aloud with a friend. One of you could read everything the goose says and does, and one of you could read what all the other animals say.

What Kind of Bird is That?

Once upon a time there lived a goose. He envied everyone and was always quarreling and hissing. "S-s-s-! S-s-s!" All the other birds and animals shook their heads and said, "My, what a very silly goose."

One day the goose saw a swan on the lake. He liked the swan's long neck. "If only I could have a neck like that!" he thought.

"Let's trade," he said to the swan. "I'll give you my neck if you will give me yours."

The swan thought it over and agreed, so they traded necks. The goose walked on with the long swan neck. A pelican passing by laughed, "You are neither goose nor swan! Ha-ha-ha!" The goose was insulted and wanted to hiss, but suddenly he noticed the pelican's large beak.

"Ah, if only I could have such a beak," thought the goose. "Let us trade," he said to the pelican.

The pelican laughed and agreed.
"How clever I am," thought the goose.
"I can get everything I ever want by trading.
I will become the finest goose in the world!"

So the goose traded his own short
legs, with their flat webbed feet, for the
crane's long legs. He traded his own large
white wings for the crow's little black
wings. He traded his short tail for the
great shimmering tail of the peacock. It
took a long time for the goose to talk the
peacock into trading, but at last the
peacock grew tired and gave in.

When the goose had nothing more to
trade, the kind-hearted rooster simply gave
him his comb and his loud "Cock-a-doodle-do!"
Now the goose looked like no other bird in
the world. He strode on the crane's long legs,
proudly waved the great peacock tail, and
turned the lovely swan neck all around.

7

Then a flock of geese landed near him.
"Ga-ga-ga! What kind of bird is that?"
they asked.

"I am a goose! I am one of you,"
he cried. He flapped the crow's wings,
stretched the swan's neck, and sang out
with the pelican's huge beak, *"Cock-a-doodle-do!* I am the most beautiful goose
in the world!"

"Well, if you are a goose, come with
us," said the geese. So he did. They came
to a field. All the geese plucked the fresh
sweet grass, but the goose could only clack
the large pelican's beak. The beak was made
for catching fish, not for eating grass.

Then the geese went to the lake to swim,
but the goose could only run back and forth along the bank.
You see, the crane's long legs were made for wading, not for
swimming. "Ga-ga-ga!" laughed the geese. *"Cock-a-doodle-do!"*
answered the goose.

The geese came out of the water. Suddenly a fox jumped
out of the reeds. The geese spread their wings and flew up
into the air. Only the goose stayed on the ground below.
The crow's little wings could not lift him up. He started
running on the crane's legs, but the peacock's tail got tangled
in the reeds. The fox caught him by the long swan's neck.

Just then the other geese came flying from all directions. They beat the fox with their wings and pecked at him with their beaks. The fox let the goose go and ran for dear life.

"Oh! Thank you for saving me," said the grateful goose. "Now I know what I must do." He went to the swan and gave him back his long neck. He returned the large beak to the pelican, and the long legs to the crane. He gave the little black wings back to the crow, the shimmering tail back to the peacock, and the comb and "*Cock-a-doodle-do*" back to the kind-hearted rooster.

He became a goose like all the other geese, but now he was wiser and kinder and he never envied anyone again.

This next story comes from African Americans in the United States. Even though this story and the first story come from places in the world that are far apart, they are alike in what they say about people.

The Knee-High Man

Once upon a time there was a knee-high man. He was no taller than a person's knees. Because he was so short, he was very unhappy. He wanted to be big like everybody else.

One day he decided to ask the biggest animal he could find how he could get big. So he went to see Mr. Horse. "Mr. Horse, how can I get big like you?"

Mr. Horse said, "Well, eat a whole lot of corn. Then run around a lot. After a while you'll be as big as me."

The knee-high man did just that. He ate so much corn that his stomach hurt. Then he ran and ran until his legs hurt. But he didn't get any bigger. So he decided that Mr. Horse had told him something wrong. He decided to go ask Mr. Bull.

"Mr. Bull? How can I get big like you?"

Mr. Bull said, "Eat a whole lot of grass. Then bellow

and bellow as loud as you can. The first thing you know, you'll be as big as me."

So the knee-high man ate a whole field of grass. That made his stomach hurt. He bellowed and bellowed and bellowed all day and all night. That made his throat hurt. But he didn't get any bigger. So he decided that Mr. Bull was all wrong too.

Now he didn't know anyone else to ask. One night he heard Mr. Hoot Owl hooting, and he remembered that Mr. Owl knew everything. "Mr. Owl? How can I get big like Mr. Horse and Mr. Bull?"

11

"What do you want to be big for?" Mr. Hoot Owl asked.

"I want to be big so that when I get into a fight, I can whip everybody," the knee-high man said.

Mr. Hoot Owl hooted. "Anybody ever try to pick a fight with you?"

The knee-high man thought a minute. "Well, now that you mention it, nobody ever did try to start a fight with me."

Mr. Owl said, "Well, you don't have any reason to fight. Therefore, you don't have any reason to be bigger than you are."

"But, Mr. Owl," the knee-high man said, "I want to be big so I can see far into the distance."

Mr. Hoot Owl hooted. "If you climb a tall tree, you can see into the distance from the top."

The knee-high man was quiet for a minute. "Well, I hadn't thought of that."

Mr. Hoot Owl hooted again. "And that's what's wrong, Mr. Knee-High Man. You hadn't done any thinking at all. I'm smaller than you, and you don't see me worrying about being big. Mr. Knee-High Man, you wanted something that you didn't need."

Do you know the story of *Little Red Riding Hood?* The next two tales are different versions of that story. The first is a Chinese story and the second is African-American.

The Chinese Red Riding Hoods

Many years ago in China there lived a young widow with her three children. The children's grandmother lived in another village. On the grandmother's birthday, the mother went to visit her.

Before she left she warned her oldest daughter, "Felice, you must watch over your sisters Mayling and Jeanne while I am gone. Lock the door and don't let anyone in. I will be back tomorrow."

A wolf hiding near the house at the edge of the woods overheard the news. When it was dark, he dressed himself as an old woman and knocked at the door.

"Who is it?" called Felice.

"Felice, Mayling, and Jeanne, my treasures, it is your Grammie," answered the wolf as sweetly as he could.

"Grammie," said Felice through the door, "Mother just went to see you!"

"It is too bad I missed her. We must have taken different roads," said the clever wolf. "Please let me in."

"Grammie," asked Felice, "why is your voice so different tonight?"

"Your old Grammie caught a cold. Please let me in quickly, for the night air is very bad for me."

They unlocked the door and shouted, "Oh Grammie, Grammie! Come in!"

As soon as the wolf got through the door, he blew out the candle saying the light hurt his tired eyes. Felice pulled out a chair and Mayling and Jeanne sat down on the wolf's lap.

"What nice, plump children!" said the wolf. "But Grammie is tired now and so are you. Time for bed." The children begged as usual to sleep in the big bed with their Grammie.

All tucked in and cozy, Mayling suddenly asked, "Grammie, what are those sharp things I feel?"

"Go to sleep, dear, those are just Grammie's nails."

Quickly, Felice lit a candle and saw the wolf's hairy face before he could blow it out. Frightened, she grabbed hold of Jeanne and said, "Grammie, Jeanne is thirsty. She needs to get a glass of water."

"Oh, for goodness sake," said the wolf, losing patience. "Wait until later." But Felice pinched Jeanne so that she started to cry.

"All right," said the wolf. "Get up Jeanne."

Felice thought fast. "Mayling," she said, "go along and help Jeanne. Oh, Grammie, have you ever tasted our delicious gingko nuts? The meat of the gingko nut is more tasty than fairy food."

"Where can I get some?" asked the wolf, drooling.

"They grow on trees outside our house. Grammie, dear, I can pick some for you," said Felice sweetly. "I'll do it right now!" said Felice, leaping out of bed.

Felice grabbed Mayling and Jeanne and ran. All three climbed the tallest gingko tree they could find. The wolf waited and waited. Finally, he went outside and called, "Felice, Mayling, Jeanne, where are you?"

"We're up in the tree eating gingko nuts," answered Felice.

"Throw some nuts down for me," yelled the wolf.

"Ah, Grammie, you will just have to climb up here to get them." The wolf now was raging with anger.

Then Felice had an idea. "Grammie, there is a clothes basket by the door with a long rope in it. Tie one end of the rope to the handle and throw the other end up to me. You get in the basket and we will pull you up."

Happily the wolf did as he was told. Felice pulled hard on the rope. Just when the basket was halfway up, she let go. Down came the wolf, badly bruised.

"Don't cry, Sister," said Mayling. "I'll help you!" So the wolf got back into the basket. They pulled with all their might. Then, part of the way up, they let go of the rope again and down came the wolf. CRASH!

"Grammie, Grammie, please don't be so upset," begged Jeanne. "All three of us will pull you up this time."

"All right, but mind you be very careful or . . . I WILL BITE YOUR HEADS OFF!" screeched the wolf. So this time all three children pulled the basket up

v-e-r-y slowly. "Heave ho, heave ho!" they sang. When the wolf was about thirty feet off the ground, Felice coughed and everyone let go of the rope! BOOM! The basket spun around and came crashing down.

The wolf let out his last howl. It was the very last howl he was ever to howl.

"Grammie! Oh Grammie!" the girls called. Hearing no answer, they slid down the tree, ran into the house, latched the door and fell fast asleep. Sweet Dreams!

As you read this story, you will find some words that are not spelled in the usual way. They are written the way people in different parts of the country say them.

A Wolf and Little Daughter

One day Little Daughter was pickin some flowers. There was a fence around the house she lived in with her papa. Papa didn't want Little Daughter to run in the forest, where there were wolves. He told Little Daughter never to go out the gate alone.

"Oh, I won't, Papa," said Little Daughter.

One mornin her papa had to go away for somethin. And Little Daughter thought she'd go huntin for flowers. She just thought it wouldn't harm anythin to peep through the gate. And that's what she did. She saw a wild yellow flower so near to the gate that she stepped outside and picked it.

Little Daughter was outside the fence now. She saw another pretty flower. She skipped over and got it, held it in her hand. It smelled sweet. She saw another and she got it too. Put it with the others. She was makin a pretty bunch to put in her vase for the table. And so Little Daughter got farther and farther away from the cabin. She picked the flowers, and the whole time she sang a sweet song.

All at once Little Daughter heard a noise. She looked up and saw a great big wolf. The wolf said to her, in a low, gruff voice, said, "Sing that sweetest, goodest song again."

So the little child sang it, "*Tray-bla, tray-bla, cum qua, kimo.*"

And, *pit-a-pat, pit-a-pat, pit-a-pat, pit-a-pat,* Little Daughter tiptoed toward the gate. She's goin back home. But she hears big and heavy, *PIT-A-PAT, PIT-A-PAT,* comin behind her. And there's the wolf. He says, "Did you move?" in a gruff voice.

Little Daughter says, "Oh, no, dear wolf, what occasion have I to move?"

"Well, sing that sweetest, goodest song again," says the wolf.

Little Daughter sang it: "*Tray-bla, tray-bla, cum qua, kimo.*"

And the wolf is gone again.

19

The child goes back some more, *pit-a-pat, pit-a-pat, pit-a-pat*, softly on tippy-toes toward the gate. But she soon hears very loud, *PIT-A-PAT, PIT-A-PAT*, comin behind her.

And there is the great big wolf, and he says to her says, "I think you moved."

"Oh, no, dear wolf," Little Daughter tells him, "what occasion have I to move?"

So he says, "Sing that sweetest, goodest song again."

Little Daughter begins: *"Tray-bla, tray-bla, tray-bla cum qua, kimo."*

The wolf is gone.

But, *PIT-A-PAT, PIT-A-PAT, PIT-A-PAT* comin on behind her. There's the wolf. He says to her, says "You moved."

She says, "Oh, no, dear wolf, what occasion have I to move?"

"Sing that sweetest, goodest song again," says the big, bad wolf.

She sang: *"Tray bla-tray, tray bla-tray, tray-bla-cum qua, kimo."*

The wolf is gone again.

And she, Little Daughter, *pit-a-pat, pit-a-pat, pit-a-pat*tin away home. She is so close to the gate now. And this time she hears *PIT-A-PAT, PIT-A-PAT, PIT-A-PAT*, comin on *quick* behind her.

Little Daughter slips inside the gate. She shuts it— CRACK! PLICK!—right in that big, bad wolf's face.

She sweetest, goodest safe!

20

Here's an African story about a deer who was afraid of a snail. Imagine! Isn't it strange that such a big animal should be afraid of such a little one? This story was made up to explain *how it came to be.* Stories that tell how or why things came to be, are called *origin myths.*

The Deer and the Snail

One day, Deer said to Snail, "I can run faster than you can."

"You cannot," replied Snail. "I may look small, but you can't tell what someone can do by the way he looks. You can't beat me in a race."

"Oh yes I can," said Deer.

"What will you give me if I can beat you?" asked Snail without any fear. He had a plan for winning the race.

"Let's see who can be the first to run to the town across the plain," said Deer. "If you lose, you and all the other snails will be servants of the deer forever. If I lose, all the other deer and I will be servants of the snails."

"I agree," said Snail. "Let it be so!" So Snail went and told all his people about the race. He also told them that he had a plan for winning, "All snails look very much alike," he said. "We will fool the deer. I'll *start* the race, but I won't be the one to finish it!"

"Who then will finish the race?" asked Snail's family.

"Here is my plan. You, Brother, will go to the bank of the first river and wait there. You, Sister, will go to the bank of the second river and wait there. You, Uncle will go to the bank of the third river and wait there. And you, Aunt, will go to the very end of the race and wait there! All of you will pretend to be me."

"What a clever fellow!" cheered Snail's family.

The day of the race arrived. Deer and Snail began. About a mile away from the start of the race, Deer came to a river. Who do you suppose was there? Snail's brother!

He cried out, "I am here already Deer, and you must carry me across!"

"All right, Snail," said Deer surprised to see the snail. "But I have not really started to run yet. Hop onto my horns!"

"Hop indeed!" said Snail's brother. "I am a crawler, not a hopper!"

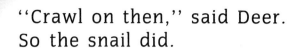

"Crawl on then," said Deer. So the snail did.

Deer ran to the next river. Snail's sister was already there. She cried out, "Deer, I am here too and you must carry me across."

Dear was really very kind. "All right, Snail," he said and carried Snail's sister across. Then he said, "I see I must run fast to beat you, Snail."

"Yes indeed!" said Snail's sister. "Run you must." So Deer began to run as fast as he could.

When he got to the next river, who do you suppose was there waiting? Right! Snail's uncle! He complained, "I have been here a long time, Deer. What have you been doing for so long? You must carry me across again."

So the kind deer carried him across. Then Deer started on his last run to the town. He ran and ran as fast as he could run. At last, all tired out, he reached the town, and he saw Snail's aunt already there. But of course, he was sure it was Snail himself.

Deer cried out and ran away. Can you imagine how he felt? He did not even wait for the judge to name the winner of the race. And ever since that day, whenever a deer sees a snail he is afraid and he runs away.

This is another origin myth from Africa. Read how a very tricky spider outwits himself.

How Spider Got a Thin Waist

Many dry seasons ago, before the oldest man in our village can remember, Spider was a very big person. He did not look as he looks today, with his fat head and his fat body and his thin waist in between. Of course, he had two eyes and eight legs and he lived in a web. But none of him was thin. He was big and round, and his waist was very fat indeed. Today, he is very different, as all of you know, and this is how it came to pass.

One day Spider was walking through the forest. It was early morning and he noticed an unusually pleasant smell. He wrinkled his nose and sniffed the wind. It was food! Goodness! He had almost forgotten. Today was the festival of the harvest. Every village in the big forest was preparing a feast. The women were cooking yams and cassava, and chicken with peanut-flavored sauce. There would be fish and peppers and rice boiling in the great pots over the fires.

Spider's heart jumped for joy. His mouth watered. His eyes sparkled and he smiled brightly. Already he could taste the food on his tongue.

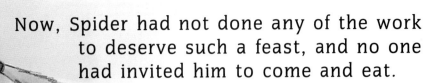

Now, Spider had not done any of the work to deserve such a feast, and no one had invited him to come and eat. Spider had not planted yam or potato. He had not planted rice, nor gone to sea in a long boat to catch fish. For Spider did not like to work at all. All day he played in the sun or slept, and since it is not the custom to refuse food to anyone who comes to one's door, he could eat very well by simply visiting all his friends.

Now spider was right in the middle of the forest. Not far away there were two villages. Spider stood just in the middle, and the two were exactly the same distance away. Today each village would have a great feast.

"How lucky for me!" thought Spider.

But then he was puzzled. Since there were two dinners, he did not know which one he wanted to go to. That is, he did not know which would have the most to eat. So Spider sat under a breadfruit tree and thought and thought and thought. At last he had an idea! He could go to them both! Of course. Spider was so pleased with his good idea that he did a little dance right there and then.

But how could he know when the food was ready? He sat under the breadfruit tree again and thought and thought and thought. And then he did two things. First, he called his eldest son, Kuma. He took a long rope and tied one end around his own waist. The other end he gave to his son. "Take this rope to the village on the East," he said to Kuma. "When the food is ready, give the rope a hard pull, and I will know it is time for me to come and eat." And so Kuma went to the East village and took the end of the rope with him.

Then Spider called his youngest son, Kwaku. He took another long rope and tied it around his waist, just below the first one. "Kwaku, take this rope to the village on the West, and when the food is all cooked, pull very hard on it. Then I will come and have my fill." So Kwaku went to the West village, carrying the end of the rope with him.

My friends, can you imagine what happened? I don't think so, so I will tell you. The people in the East village and the people in the West village had their dinners at exactly the same time. So, of course, Kuma and Kwaku pulled on both of the ropes at the same time. Kuma pulled to the East and Kwaku pulled to the West. The ropes got tighter and tighter. Poor, greedy Spider was caught in the middle.

Kuma and Kwaku could not understand why their father did not come, and they pulled harder all the time. And something was happening to Spider. The ropes squeezed tighter and tighter and his waist got thinner and thinner. Kuma and Kwaku waited until all the food was eaten. Then they came to look for their father. When they found him, he looked very different. His waist line was thinner than a needle! Spider never grew fat again. He stayed the same until today. He has a big head and a big body, and a tiny little waist in between.

26

You've read about outwitting yourself. Can you imagine out-wishing yourself? As you read this Spanish folk tale, you will see that sometimes wishes can get you into trouble. Have you discovered that?

The Three Wishes

Once upon a time, there was a young married couple. They lived in a little house called a *bohío*. Around the *bohío* was a field of peas, called *gandules*. They often ate the *gandules* for their meals, for they didn't have much else to eat. They were poor, but really quite happy. Not far from their home was a forest. Here the husband cut firewood to sell at the market.

One day the wife was boiling a pot of *gandules* for dinner. A knock came at the door. She went to answer it. There stood an old man with a beard.

"*Buenos días, Señora,*" he said. "Is your husband in?"

"*Buenos días, Señor,*" said the woman. "My husband is at the market selling firewood. Come in and rest. He will be home very soon."

The old man went in and sat on the small stool she gave him. He looked around.

"You must be very poor," said the man.

"That we are," replied the woman. "But life has been good to us. Every day we give thanks for our gifts."

The old man smiled. "That's why I have been sent here to grant you three wishes. You have but to ask, and your wishes will be granted."

Now while they were talking, the woman had been stirring the pot of *gandules* with a rough, flat stick. A wonderful thought came to her.

"Ay, *Señor*," she cried, "give me a *cucharón*, a large ladle that I can use to stir my *gandules.*"

No sooner said than done. The woman found herself holding a beautiful *cucharón*. She was overjoyed! She was about to ask for something else, when the door opened and her husband came in. He stared at the stranger sitting on the stool, and wondered what he was doing there. His wife said, "Oh husband, be happy. The *señor* came to grant us three wishes. It's really so, husband. I asked for a *cucharón* and look, here it is!"

The husband flew into a rage. "Silly, silly wife," he shouted. "You have wasted a good wish on such a little thing. You showed no more sense than a burro, my wife. I wish that the *cucharón* were sticking in the middle of your back!"

No sooner said than done. The *cucharón* jumped from her hands and stuck right in the middle of her back. The woman tried to pull it off, but she could not reach it. She jumped and twisted and hopped trying to shake it off, but it would not move.

The old man stood up. "It is getting late," he said quietly. "Would someone care to ask for the last wish?"

The wife looked at her husband. It was a look like no other look her husband had ever seen. Her eyes filled with tears. He had never seen her look so unhappy. It was more than he could bear. "Let the *cucharón* return to my wife's hands," he said quickly. No sooner said than done. And there stood his wife, smiling and holding the beautiful *cucharón*.

They turned to thank the old man, but he had disappeared.

This English version of the wishing story is like the Spanish one, but in some ways it's a flip-flop of that tale. Puzzled? Read on.

The Three Wishes

Once upon a time, and be sure it was a long time ago, there lived a poor woodman in a great forest. Every day of his life he went out to chop wood. One day he started out with his pack. His good wife had filled it with meat and drink for his day in the forest. Some time before he had marked a huge old oak tree. He thought he could get many good planks of wood from it.

When he came to the tree, he took his axe in his hand and swung it round his head. But he hadn't given one blow, when he heard the saddest cry. There, before him, stood a fairy who begged him to save the tree. He was dazed with wonder and fear and couldn't open his mouth to speak a word. He found his tongue at last, and said, "I'll do as you wish. The tree will stand."

"You've done better for yourself than you know," answered the fairy. "And to show I'm grateful, I'll give you three wishes, be they

what they may." And from
then on the fairy was seen
no more.

The woodman slung his
pack over his shoulder and
started home. But the way
was long, and the poor man
was dazed with the wonderful
thing that had happened to
him. When he got home, there
was nothing in his noodle but
the need to sit down and rest.
Maybe, too, it was a fairy's
trick. Who can tell? Anyway,
down he sat by the blazing
fire, and as he sat he became
very hungry.

"Have you nothing yet for
supper, wife?" said he.

"Nay, not for a couple of
hours," said she.

31

"Ah!" groaned the woodman, "I wish I had a good link of sausage here before me."

No sooner had he said the words, when— CLATTER, CLATTER, RUSTLE, RUSTLE— what should come down the chimney but a link of the finest sausage any man could wish for. If the woodman stared, the good wife stared three times as much. "What's all this?" says she.

Then the woodman told her the tale of his morning from the beginning to end. As he told it the good wife was getting angrier by the second. And when he had finished she burst out, "You are nothing but a fool! I wish the sausage would stick to your nose. I do indeed!"

And before you could say Jack Robinson, there the good man sat with his nose grown longer with a fine link of sausage stuck to it! He gave the sausage a pull, but it stuck. And she gave it a pull, but it stuck. And they both pulled and pulled until they had nearly pulled his nose off! Still the sausage stuck and stuck.

"What's to be done now?" said he.

"Well, it isn't so *very* ugly to look at," said she, looking hard at him.

Then the woodman understood that if he wished, he would have to wish in a hurry! And wish he did, that the sausage would come off his nose.

Well it did! There it lay in a dish on the table. Even if the good man and his good wife didn't get to ride in a golden coach, or dress in silk and satin, they at least had as fine a sausage for their supper as any man could wish for.

In this African-American tale you meet Brer Rabbit. He is one of the world's greatest tricksters. In this story Brer Rabbit hears a noise and keeps his feelings about it a secret. Why do you think he did? This tale also has some unusual words.

The Noise in the Woods

Brer Rabbit was meandering through the woods one day when he heard Mr. Man chopping down a tree. Brer Rabbit stopped to listen. All of a sudden— KUBBER-LANG-BANG-BLAM!

Brer Rabbit jumped up in the air and took off running. Now, Brer Rabbit might try to claim he wasn't scared, but it's just like lightning and thunder. Folks know that thunder can't hurt 'em but when a loud clap of it come, they get scared and want to run anyhow. Well, that's the way it was with Brer Rabbit that morning. He ran and he ran and he ran some more, until he was almost out of breath. And about then, Brer Coon came along.

"What's your hurry, Brer Rabbit?"

"Ain't got no time to tarry."

"Is your folks sick?"

"No, thank God. Ain't got no time to tarry!"

"Well, what's the matter?"

"Mighty big racket back there in the woods. Ain't got no time to tarry!"

Brer Coon got kinna skittish because he was a long ways away from home. He took off running and hadn't gone far when he run smack dab into Brer Fox.

"Brer Coon! Where are you going?"

"Ain't got no time to tarry."

"Is your folks sick?"

"No, thank God. Ain't got no time to tarry!"

"Well, what's the matter, Brer Coon?"

"Mighty queer noise back there in the woods. Ain't got no time to tarry!"

And Brer Fox split the wind. He hadn't gone far when he run smack dab into Brer Wolf.

"Brer Fox! Stop and rest yourself!"

"Ain't got no time to tarry!"

"Is your folks sick?"

"No thank God. Ain't got no time to tarry!"

"Well, good or bad, Brer Fox. Tell me the news!"

"There's a mighty noise back there in the woods. Ain't got no time to tarry!"

Brer Wolf scratched earth getting away from there. He hadn't gone far before he ran into Brer Bear. Brer Bear asked him what was wrong and Brer Wolf told him about the mighty noise. Brer Bear might have been big but he wasn't slow and he shook the earth getting away. Before long every animal in the community was running like Ole Boy was after them.

They ran and they ran until they came to Brer Turtle's house. Being about out of breath by this time, they stopped to rest. Brer Turtle wanted to know what all the excitement was.

"Mighty noise back there in the woods," Brer Fox said.

"What it sound like?"

None of them knew.

"Who heard the racket?" Brer Turtle asked.

They asked one another and found out that none of them had.

Brer Turtle chuckled. "Excuse me, gentlemen. Believe it's time for me to go eat my breakfast." And he left.

The animals inquired among each other. They weren't surprised to discover that Brer Rabbit was the one what started the news about the noise.

They went over to his house one sunny afternoon and he was sitting on the porch, getting a tan.

"What you trying to make a fool of me for?" Brer Bear spoke up.

"Fool of who, Brer Bear?"

"Me, Brer Rabbit! That's who."

"This is the first time I've seen you today, Brer Bear."

Brer Coon spoke up. "Well, you seen me today, and you made a fool of me."

"How I fool you?"

"You pretended like there was a big racket in the woods, Brer Rabbit."

"Wasn't no pretend. There was a big racket in the woods."

"What kind?" Brer Coon asked.

Brer Rabbit chuckled. "You ought to ask me that first, Brer Coon. Wasn't nothing but Mr. Man cutting down a tree. If you'd asked me, I would've told you. Sho' would have." And he turned his face up to the sun, closed his eyes, a big smile on his face.

The catbird in this Hopi Indian story had good reasons for not following the rules. Find out what they were.

Mockingbird Gives Out the Calls

In the beginning of things the birds were brought to life, but only Yaalpa, the mockingbird, had the knowledge of speech. It was the mockingbird who gave languages to the people when they emerged from the Lower World, and now he decided that the creatures of the air should also have a way of speaking. So one day he called them all together for a meeting.

He said, "All the tribes of men have their languages. When a Hopi speaks, it is with a Hopi voice. When an Apache speaks, you know him by the sound of his words. When a Navaho speaks, you know him to be a Navaho. The birds also should have languages. Since I am the one who has the knowledge of languages, I will give you the calls by which you will be recognized."

He addressed the rock hen, saying, "You, rock hen, your call shall be 'Chew! Chew! Chew!' Whenever you wish to announce your presence, you will say, 'Chew! Chew! Chew!' And whenever I want you to attend a meeting, I will call you by that sound."

The rock hen tried out his call, "Chew! Chew! Chew!" Then he flew off quickly, saying, "That's all I have to know."

Mockingbird spoke then to the red-tailed hawk. "You, red-tailed hawk, you will call out shrilly like this: 'Sieuuuu! Sieuuuu! Sieuuuu!'"

"I hear what you say," the red-tailed hawk said. He tried out his call, *"Sieuuuu! Sieuuuu! Sieuuuu!"* And then he departed.

The mockingbird addressed the dove. "You, dove, you shall make a soft call like this: *'Hu-hu-huuu! Hu-hu-huuu!'*"

"Hu-hu-huuu! Hu-hu-huuu!" the dove said, and he flew away.

"You, owl," the mockingbird said, "you are to make a sound in your throat like this: *'G-hew! G-hew! G-hew!'*"

"Yes, I have it," the owl said. He, also, went away.

The mockingbird continued giving out calls, and as each bird learned what he was to say, he went home. Finally only the catbird remained. The mockingbird looked at him. He was surprised, for the two of them looked very much alike. "We appear to be cousins," the mockingbird said. "What kind of bird are you?"

"Yes," the catbird answered, "I am easily mistaken for you. I am the catbird."

"Well," the mockingbird said, "I will give you your call."

"No," the catbird said, "I don't think I want any call."

"Every bird should have its call," the mockingbird said.

"In this case it is different," the catbird answered. "From what I have seen, you are not very popular with the other birds. You are talking all the time. Too much talking drives people away. Did you notice how the birds left the meeting as soon as they could? They avoid you. You talk too much. I would rather not have a language. If I talk, the other birds may think I am you."

"But if I want to hold a meeting," the mockingbird said, "you will have to know your special call."

"No, it won't be necessary," the catbird replied. "If I hear you calling out 'G-hew!' for the owl and 'Sieuuuu!' for the red-tailed hawk, then I will know there is to be a meeting and I will come."

"But," the mockingbird said, "how will you announce your presence when you arrive?"

"I'll just flutter my wings," the catbird said, and he flew away.

This is why the catbird says practically nothing. The only sound he makes is a faint "*Miem!*" He was ashamed of his cousin, the mockingbird, who talked too much, and when the calls were given out, he refused to accept one for himself.

This next tale comes from Burma, a country in Asia. In it, the mice are looking for a strong and powerful bridegroom for Miss Mouse. Do they find one?

Miss Mouse Finds a Bridegroom

Once upon a time there was a little mouse who was so sweet and beautiful that her parents thought she was the most wonderful daughter on earth. When the time came for her to be married, they couldn't find a bridegroom good enough for her. So, they went to see the sun.

"Oh, mighty Sun," they said, "you are the most powerful being there is. So, you are worthy to become the bridegroom of our sweet and beautiful daughter."

"I will gladly become the bridegroom of your sweet and beautiful daughter," said the sun, "but there is another who has greater power than I. There is one who has the power to force me from the sky. I mean, of course, the rain."

"Of course, the rain!" said Mr. and Mrs. Mouse. "Thank you." So they went to find the rain.

"Oh, mighty Rain," they said, "you can force the sun from the sky. You are a fitting bridegroom for our sweet and beautiful daughter. Will *you* marry her?"

"I am honored," replied the rain, "but there is one far more powerful. The wind who pushes me is mightier than I." So Mr. and Mrs. Mouse went to find the wind.

"Oh, mighty Wind," they said, "you push away the rain. You are a fitting bridegroom for our sweet and beautiful daughter. Will *you* marry her?"

"Marry her?" said the wind, "I would be glad to! However, there is one far more powerful than I. It is the mountain who stands in my way." So Mr. and Mrs. Mouse went to find the mountain.

"Oh, mighty Mountain," they said, "you can stop even the wind. Will you become the bridegroom of our sweet and beautiful daughter? Will *you* marry her?"

"Yes, indeed," replied the mountain. "However, I must tell you that there is one far more powerful than I. It is the bull who sharpens his great horns against me and breaks me into bits. He is mightier than I." So Mr. and Mrs. Mouse went to find the bull.

"Oh, Bull," they said, "you can turn the mountain to dust. You are a fitting bridegroom for our sweet and beautiful daughter. Will *you* marry her?"

"I am a mighty animal," said the bull, "but the rope is my master. It pulls me from left to right."

"Then we will find the rope," said Mr. and Mrs. Mouse. So they did.

"Oh, Rope, you rule the bull. You are a fitting bridegroom for our sweet and beautiful daughter. Will *you* marry her?"

"I am sometimes strong, but often weak. Every night the mouse who lives in the cowshed, comes and gnaws at me. He is the one who makes me weak. See him."

So Mr. and Mrs. Mouse went to find the mouse who lived in the cowshed. They saw right away that he was a wonderful fellow. He was *thrilled* to marry someone as sweet and beautiful as Miss Mouse. So at last a fitting bridegroom was found, and he and Miss Mouse were married and lived happily ever after.

This tale is told in Puerto Rico. It is a story that g-r-o-w-s each time a new character is added. Now think about this. Is the ending to this story sad or silly? It just might be both!

The Bed

There was once a little old woman who had a little boy. She brought him up under an old-fashioned bed.

But when the bed squeaked, the little boy was afraid and cried, "Booh, Booh."

The little old woman ran to him and said, "Don't cry little boy. It's only the sound of this old-fashioned bed."

And this same little old woman bought a little dog, and gave it to the little boy for company.

But when the bed squeaked, the dog barked, "Wow, Wow."

The boy cried, "Booh, Booh."

The little old woman ran to them and said, "Don't bark, little dog. Don't cry, little boy. It's only the sound of this old-fashioned bed."

45

And this same little old woman bought a little cat and gave it to the boy for company.

But when the bed squeaked, the cat said, "Miaow, Miaow."

The dog barked, "Wow, Wow."

The boy said, "Booh, Booh."

The little old woman ran to them and said, "Don't miaow, little cat. Don't bark, little dog. Don't cry, little boy. It's only the sound of this old-fashioned bed."

Now this same little old woman bought a little mouse and gave it to the boy for company.

But when the bed squeaked, the mouse cried, "Chui, Chui."

The cat said, "Miaow, Miaow."

The dog barked, "Wow, Wow."

The boy said, "Booh, Booh."

The little old woman ran to them and said, "Don't squeak, little mouse. Don't miaow, little cat. Don't bark, little dog. Don't cry, little boy. It's only the sound of this old-fashioned bed."

And this same little old woman bought a little pig, and gave it to the boy for company.

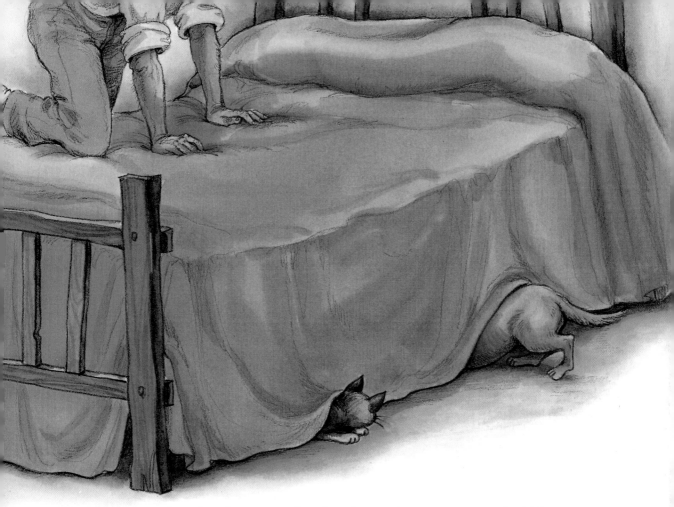

But when the bed squeaked, the pig screamed, "Grunt, Grunt."

The mouse squeaked, "Chui, Chui."

The cat said, "Miaow, Miaow."

The dog barked, "Wow, Wow."

The boy cried, "Booh, Booh."

The little old woman ran to them and said, "Don't grunt, little pig. Don't squeak, little mouse. Don't miaow, little cat. Don't bark, little dog. Don't cry, little boy. It's only the sound of this old-fashioned bed."

Then one day her little old man came home and stretched out to rest on the old-fashioned bed.

But when the bed squeaked, he cried, "Ah, Meeeeee."

The pig screamed, "Grunt, Grunt."

The mouse squeaked, "Chui, Chui."

The cat said, "Miaow, Miaow."

The dog barked, "Wow, Wow."

The boy cried, "Booh, Booh."

The little old woman ran to them and said, "Don't grumble, old man. Don't grunt, little pig. Don't squeak, little mouse. Don't miaow, little cat. Don't bark, little dog. Don't cry, little boy. It's only the sound of this old-fashioned bed."

At just that moment——the old bed BROKE DOWN!

The old man fell out.

And it bruised the little pig.

And it pinched the little mouse.

And it scratched the little cat,

But the little dog escaped.

And the little boy was saved. Hurray! Hurrah!

And the little old woman was so very brave that she just sat on the floor and laughed until she shook.